THE PERCEPTION

BRING IT TO LIGHT

AKASH

Contents

Preface

Some people believe that everything in life is temporary, yet when faced with even a small difficulty, they feel as though their entire world is falling apart. The key to making our dreams come true lies in what we understand within ourselves. This book is not meant to simply motivate you, because motivation gained from external sources—whether from books, speakers, music, friends, or movies—tends to be short-lived. Don't expect someone from outside will motivate you. That's not a permanent solution. Look into yourself.

Human perception is the process by which we interpret and make sense of the world around us. It acts as the bridge between reality and our understanding of it, enabling us to navigate life by transforming sensory input—sights, sounds, smells, tastes, and touch—into meaningful experiences. Yet, perception is far more complex and profound than simply sensing the environment; it is deeply intertwined with our thoughts, emotions, memories, and beliefs.

Perception is not flawless. Optical illusions, biases, and cognitive distortions reveal how our minds can misinterpret reality. Our brains often "fill in the blanks" to create coherent narratives, even when we lack complete information. This can lead to false assumptions and flawed judgments.

Despite its limitations, perception is incredibly powerful. It shapes how we respond to challenges, how we connect with others, and how we view ourselves. By becoming aware of how perception works, we can challenge our assumptions, expand our understanding, and change our outlook on life.

Perception is not just about seeing the world as it is but about creating the world we want to see. It reminds us that while reality may be objective, our experience of it is uniquely ours—a dynamic interplay of mind, body, and environment. By cultivating awareness of our perceptions, we gain the ability to better understand ourselves, empathize with others, and approach life with clarity and purpose.

Perception is the unseen lens through which we experience life. It shapes our understanding of the world, guides our choices, and influences the paths we follow. This silent force, often operating in the background, has a profound impact on our thoughts, emotions, and actions. Perception is not simply about what we see—it's about how we see, how we interpret the people we meet, the challenges we face, and the opportunities we encounter. It is the foundation of our reality, shaping the narratives we create and the truths we choose to believe.

The Perception: Bring it to Light invites you to embark on a transformative journey of self-discovery and awareness. Within these pages lies an exploration of the intricate and often hidden mechanisms of perception—how it defines our sense of self, influences our relationships, and informs our interaction with the world. This book challenges the limits of conventional thinking, prompting you to question the assumptions and norms you've unconsciously embraced. It invites you to uncover perspectives you might have overlooked and bring clarity to the shadows of your mind.

By delving into the unseen forces that shape our lives, this book encourages deep reflection, bold questioning, and a willingness to confront the unknown. It is a call to peel back the layers of perception, to question what you see, and to understand how these interpretations influence your choices and beliefs. Through this process, we open ourselves to immense personal growth, gaining the ability to see beyond illusions, think critically, and live with authenticity and purpose.

This book is more than a guide to understanding perception; it is an opportunity to transform how you engage with life. As you read, you'll uncover the power to shift your perspective, gain clarity, and illuminate new paths forward. Whether you're seeking to deepen your self-awareness, strengthen your connections with others, or find clarity amidst life's complexities, The Perception:

Bring it to Light is your companion on this remarkable journey.
Let these words inspire you to see the world with fresh eyes, embrace your true self, and bring your perception into the light.
"Lets dive into the Black Hole"

ϷϷϷ

Acknowledgements

With heartfelt gratitude, I extend my deepest thanks to everyone who contributed to the realization of The Perception: Bring it to Light. This book is as much a reflection of my journey as it is a culmination of the guidance, support, and inspiration I've received along the way.

To my family and friends—your unwavering belief in me has been my foundation. Through your encouragement, patience, and love, you have been my constant light, reminding me of the power of connection and trust. Every word of this book has been inspired by the strength you've given me.

To my mentors and teachers—you have shaped my thinking and opened my eyes to the value of curiosity and critical reflection. By encouraging me to challenge norms, delve deeper into the unseen, and embrace growth, you have left an indelible mark on my life and this work.

To the readers of this book—your willingness to embark on this journey of discovery means more than words can express. Your hunger for clarity, your bravery to question, and your openness to explore new perspectives are the driving force behind these pages. You are the heart of this endeavour, and it is my hope that this book resonates deeply with you.

Finally, to life itself—the ultimate teacher. The intricate dance of experiences, challenges, and quiet moments of revelation has been the foundation of my understanding of perception. Life's lessons—both harsh and beautiful—are woven into the fabric of this book, serving as a reminder that every moment holds the potential for profound growth.

This book is not just a personal project; it is a tribute to the power of shared wisdom, the beauty of human potential, and the endless possibilities that emerge when we dare to see the world differently. Thank you for being part of this journey, for your support, and for your trust in these pages. Let's bring perception into the light, together.

ᗐᗐᗐ

• x •

ONE

The Perception of Two Dimension

In our lives, the concept of balance is prevalent. If something we consider good exists, there must also be something we consider bad. This duality is embedded in various aspects of existence. We see it in the contrasting forces of Yin and Yang, the interplay between positive and negative, the rise and fall of movements, the juxtaposition of light and dark, and the dynamic between truth and dishonesty. These dualities are fundamental to how we understand the world and ourselves.

The fascinating thing about this duality is how different people interpret these opposites. Some may seek to live in the light, while others may find comfort in the dark. What one person perceives as a positive action, another might view as negative. For example, during the day, the sun shines brightly, symbolizing beauty, vitality, and growth. At night, the moon, though not as bright as the sun, is equally beautiful and revered in its own way, especially in literature and culture where it often represents the beauty of love. In fact, the moon's light in the night sky is a metaphor for the way we often perceive love as something that transcends darkness.

This duality also extends to our morality and choices. For instance, while we may condemn the act of killing animals, when we do so for food, it doesn't seem wrong to us. Hunting and consuming meat has been part of our evolutionary journey, ingrained in our survival instincts. While some argue that eating meat may be essential for our health, we only attain that health by ending the life of an innocent being. This paradox is a striking example of how what is considered "good" (feeding ourselves) often comes at the cost of something that is deemed "bad" (taking the life of another creature). It is through such contradictions that we begin to understand the true complexity of life.

The coexistence of good and bad is not just inevitable but essential. It is only by acknowledging what is bad or undesirable that we can truly understand what is good. This dynamic interplay between opposites defines life, where both the positive and negative aspects of existence are interdependent. The ancient concept of yin and yang beautifully captures this idea, suggesting that harmony and balance are achieved not through the absence of one force but through the dynamic interplay of both. In Hinduism, the belief that without Lord Shiva, there would be no Shakti underscores this balance. The union of the two forces is symbolized in the depiction of Arthanareeswara, a deity that embodies both masculine and feminine energies, emphasizing that both are necessary for completeness.

Our perception of the world plays a key role in how we experience life's dualities. How we interpret something often shapes our emotional response to it. For example, every star is born out of darkness, and the light eventually dispels the darkness. In this sense, darkness is not inherently bad, but a necessary condition for the birth of light—symbolizing knowledge, growth, and enlightenment.

The philosopher Plato once said, "We can easily forgive a child who is afraid of the dark; the real tragedy of life is when men are afraid of the light." This quote speaks to the human tendency to fear the unknown, especially in adulthood. While it is understandable for a child to fear what they cannot see or comprehend, it becomes tragic when adults fear the truth, knowledge, or enlightenment—the light. Light, in this metaphorical sense, represents not just physical illumination but the awareness and understanding of life's complexities, including its dualities. For adults to fear the light is to resist change, to reject new knowledge, and to be unwilling to confront the truth. The fear of the light reflects a fear of growth and transformation.

In our modern world, one of the most pervasive fears people face is the fear of negative thinking. Negative thoughts are inevitable, and they often arise when we experience opposing emotions or situations. However, it's important to realize that these thoughts do not need to dominate us. If we take a moment to reflect, we can see that many of these negative thoughts are based on past experiences or imagined future scenarios. They are often not grounded in reality.

So why do we experience such negative thoughts? One reason is that they are linked to our primal instincts for survival. We have been conditioned through centuries of evolution to perceive certain situations as threatening, and our minds generate negative thoughts as a form of caution, helping us to anticipate possible dangers. These thoughts act as mental preparation, allowing us to protect ourselves from harm. However, the challenge is not to ignore these thoughts entirely, but to understand them for what they are: mental patterns that were once useful for survival but may no longer be necessary in our modern lives.

To transform these negative thoughts into positive ones, we must first recognize their source. Are they rooted in actual events from our past? Or are they simply fear-based projections about the future? Once we understand their origins, we can begin to reframe them. By recognizing the balance between light and dark, positive and negative, we can learn to appreciate both sides and use them as opportunities for growth. In this way, the negative does not need to overpower the positive, but can be understood as part of a greater whole, contributing to the richness and depth of life.

Ultimately, the key to transforming negative thoughts lies in shifting our perspective. Just as light and dark coexist, so too can positive and negative thoughts coexist in our minds. By accepting the negative as a part of life and focusing on how we can respond to it in a constructive way, we can find the balance that leads to personal growth and greater peace of mind.

But how can we manage these negative thoughts?

In a village, there lived a wise man known for giving incredibly insightful teachings. The villagers would often visit him to listen to his words of wisdom. One day, a man came to meet the wise man. This man's mind was filled with overwhelming worries and confusion. He shared everything with the wise man. In truth, the man's main problem was that his mind was consumed with numerous negative thoughts. He was afraid that all the things he imagined might actually happen. After expressing all his fears and concerns to the wise man, he asked:

He: Master, if we say 'fire,' it doesn't burn us; if we say 'sweet,' it doesn't taste sweet to us either. So why are only these thoughts causing us distress? How can we move forward from this?

Wise Man: Can the corn cob puppet walk?

He: No!

Wise Man: Can the corn cob puppet speak?

He: No!

Wise Man: So why do crows run away in fear of it?

He: Haha... how do crows know when a corn cob doll is dead, it has its own intuition.

Wise Man: Our mind is like that; if we have not properly trained ourselves, we are afraid of the negative thought that is just an image, just like how that five-sense animal is afraid of that corn cob doll.

Take life at a distance and you will know in what dimension that beauty is.

ᗡᗡᗡ

TWO

THE PERCEPTION OF TRUST

Have you ever stopped to think about what we believe in and why we believe it? Trust is a fundamental quality for any person. Belief shapes our lives, whether we are aware of it or not, as each day passes. But are our beliefs truly our own, or are they influenced by the beliefs of others?

Belief has a significant influence on the world. Religion is a belief, God is a belief, and even the idea of Satan is a belief. This world is deeply enveloped and shaped by belief. How?

The currency notes we use every day are a powerful symbol of trust. Have you noticed? On those notes, it is written, "I promise to pay the bearer the sum of one hundred rupees." Have we ever stopped to think about what that really means? The true value of that hundred-rupee note lies in the gold reserve backing it. But in reality, does the gold physically exist in proportion to every note? No.

Yet, we continue to exchange money, believing that the value exists. Why do we hold on to this belief even when we know the gold might not actually be there? Is it because everyone else believes in it? Or is it simply because we haven't fully understood the system yet?

In India, we maintain only a minimum gold reserve, yet we continue to believe that the gold exists, which is truly remarkable! Money is just paper, but it is the trust placed in the signature of the Governor printed on it that gives it value and life.

Though money is merely paper, the belief and aspirations associated with it are vast and boundless.

Throughout history, belief has been a force that has transformed the world. Judaism, in particular, is deeply rooted in belief. The followers of Judaism believed that their central deity, the Messiah, would be reborn into this world to guide them. However, what actually happened was quite the opposite.

If the Jews had dismissed their belief as false, Christianity—now a dominant global religion, whether openly or indirectly—might never have come into existence.

Consciously or unconsciously, we place our trust in others. Many things we believe in are embedded in our lives without us even realizing it.

For instance, we go to sleep believing we will wake up the next day. When we drive a vehicle, we trust that it won't veer off the road. Similarly, when we ride with friends, we trust that they won't cause an accident. These beliefs, though subtle, shape our everyday existence.

Whenever trust is broken, our brain resists accepting the new reality. The brain operates based on established patterns created through trust, and when that pattern is suddenly disrupted, it seeks a similar replacement. If no such pattern is found, it either takes time or struggles to accept the truth.

For example, at birth, when the nurse says, "This is your mother," we believe it without question. Similarly, after birth, we accept the religion our parents identify as ours because they tell us so. But what if all these beliefs turned out to be false? Would our brain readily accept such a reality?

The human brain is truly extraordinary—both incredibly marvelous and, at times, highly precarious. We can compare our brain to the vast universe in its complexity and potential.

The word "trust" cannot encompass everything on its own. We can classify trust in many ways, and only then can we fully understand its depth and meaning.

• Emotional Trust: Emotional trust is about understanding someone's feelings and genuinely respecting them. The boundless trust given to us by our parents during our childhood is rooted in truth and selflessness, aimed at nurturing our growth. Although Alexander the Great ruled vast territories of the world with his prowess, the unparalleled trust and loyalty his close friend Hephaestion showed him remain an unsung yet pivotal force in the pages of history.

• Reliability Trust: Reliability trust is the deep confidence in someone's ability to consistently fulfill their responsibilities, keep their promises, and demonstrate trustworthy behavior. Mahatma Gandhi firmly committed to the principle of non-violence as his approach to resistance. He never wavered in his belief, and it was this unwavering trust in his principles that enabled him to unite countless people across India and make the movement both impactful and seamless.

Trust has been a cornerstone of human society for centuries, influencing how we interact, build relationships, and function as a collective. From the simplest personal relationships to larger societal frameworks, trust has always been vital. It shapes our perception of the world and our ability to navigate it confidently. However, despite some negative experiences that may cloud our judgment, trust continues to play a central role in our lives. We place trust in various aspects, whether it's in people, systems, or knowledge, and it remains a foundational element of societal functioning.

Authors, for example, rely on trust in their knowledge and experience when writing. They trust that the information they share will be valued, and that readers will accept their perspectives. This trust is not only in the material they are conveying but also in the broader human understanding and connection. Books, regardless of genre, are expressions of the trust authors place in their ability to inform, entertain, or persuade others.

Over time, however, the nature of trust has evolved. In the past, people trusted established systems and institutions with greater certainty. Religious institutions, government bodies, and authority figures were sources of guidance, and people accepted their teachings with little question. But as society progressed, and as individuals became more exposed to different worldviews, scientific advancements, and global events, trust in these traditional entities began to waver. The certainty that once accompanied trust in religion or authority has diminished in many places, and for some, it has completely eroded.

This shift in trust is also reflected in the way we approach personal relationships. In earlier times, people were more likely to trust in the institutions of marriage, family, or community as stable sources of emotional and social security. Today, however, many people question or redefine what trust means in relationships. Trust in love and long-term partnerships has been tested by societal changes, such as increasing rates of divorce, shifting gender roles, and more fluid views on relationships.

Similarly, the trust people once had in educators or institutions of learning has also shifted. While teachers and educational systems used to be seen as the ultimate authorities on knowledge, today there is a growing skepticism about formal education. People question the relevance of traditional schooling systems in an ever-changing world. Instead, some parents may choose to send their children to special classes or alternative educational models, reflecting a desire to trust systems that are seen as more adaptable or aligned with contemporary needs.

In essence, trust is a fluid concept that changes with time, culture, and experience. What was once accepted without question now requires greater scrutiny. Trust in institutions and relationships is no longer guaranteed, and it must be earned and maintained in new ways. As society continues to evolve, so too will the ways in which we place our trust, constantly reshaping the framework of our lives and interactions.

Human trust can often be a deeply rooted and powerful force. At times, this trust extends beyond just believing in others, but also in the larger flow of life and its unseen patterns. Many individuals hold a belief that even when something bad or unfortunate occurs, there is often a greater purpose behind it. This belief may be rooted in spiritual or philosophical ideas, such as the notion of fate or karma, where the universe or a higher power orchestrates events in a way that ultimately benefits us in the long run.

This strong trust in a larger plan can provide individuals with the resilience to endure difficult times. For instance, when facing setbacks or challenges, they may maintain the conviction that these hardships will lead to personal growth, greater understanding, or even unexpected opportunities down the road. Such trust becomes a coping mechanism—transforming adversity into something they can accept, learn from, or even welcome, knowing that it contributes to their larger life journey.

This trust, when internalized, allows individuals to remain adaptable. Instead of resisting change, they may embrace it, believing that their circumstances, even if painful in the moment, are leading them to a better place. It fosters a mindset of hope and positive expectation, which in turn motivates individuals to continue forward despite challenges, rather than retreating or giving up. Therefore, trust does not just serve to maintain peace of mind but also empowers people to take control of their responses to life's ups and downs, ultimately leading to personal evolution and growth.

In today's world, trust is a crucial matter. You can choose to place your trust in God, or you can place it in the systems of the world. If you choose to trust the systems of the world, they may fail you at some point. However, when you place your trust in God, He will never fail you.

What kind of trust is this for you? Trusting in something non-existent in this world!

Trust is the currency in God's kingdom. Just like currency is used as a medium of exchange, trust allows you to exchange what God has for what you have. What you bring is trust, and what God offers is everything you need for life.

Trust is a fascinating concept. We place trust in various aspects of life: in the world around us, in ourselves, in others, and even in the truth itself. "Believe that" and "Believe in" are two different expressions of trust. "Believe that" means accepting something as true based on knowledge, while "Believe in" means trusting others. If someone tells you that you should not trust someone else, we often question that. It may not necessarily be that their words are invalid, but we need to reflect on why they say that and consider if their advice holds value in our understanding.

If the human perspective is limited, we place trust in something, but we wonder if our trust is truly correct and whether it is based on the right understanding.

When trust is intertwined with our struggles, we often encounter painful truths. If you are...

ppp

THREE

THE PERCEPTION OF FEAR

Fear is a common experience shared by all living beings in this world. We all encounter fear in some form every day.

So, what exactly is fear? How can we understand it better?

By examining how it affects our lives, we can find ways to overcome its grip and learn how to manage it.

Why does fear arise in us?

When something unexpected occurs that has the potential to harm us, our natural instinct is to become alert and cautious. This response is not arbitrary but is deeply ingrained in our biology and psychology. From an evolutionary standpoint, our ancestors developed this heightened sense of awareness to protect themselves from immediate dangers, such as predators or environmental hazards. In many ways, this ingrained survival mechanism is still active today, guiding our reactions to new threats, even in a world that may no longer present the same physical dangers.

Over time, this instinct to respond quickly to perceived danger has become a learned behavior. We condition ourselves to stay vigilant in the face of uncertainty, making split-second decisions about how to protect our safety and well-being. This way of thinking has been passed down through generations, creating a mental framework that helps us anticipate and react to potential threats.

Our brains are wired to prioritize survival, and this is reflected in the way we react to the unknown.

When we encounter something that we perceive as a threat—whether it's an actual physical danger or simply a scenario that evokes fear—we immediately begin to prepare ourselves. This is a mental process that often involves anticipating worst-case scenarios and coming up with strategies to address the problem. This reaction can be linked to what is known in scientific terms as a "phobia." A phobia is an irrational fear that becomes activated when we think about or encounter something we consider threatening. It is the body's way of preparing to handle perceived danger, but it is often disproportionate to the actual threat.

The active role of fear in this process is both protective and problematic. On the one hand, fear helps us take precautionary actions to avoid danger. On the other hand, when we dwell on potential problems or imagined threats, we can experience anxiety or panic that may not be justified by the situation at hand. This is where exaggeration comes into play. While our fear response is intended to protect us, it can often lead us to overestimate the likelihood of a threat or misinterpret a situation. We may spend excessive amounts of time worrying about things that are either highly unlikely to happen or entirely disconnected from the actual danger.

For example, we might feel fearful of an upcoming presentation, thinking it will result in failure or embarrassment, even though the likelihood of that outcome is low. This kind of thinking can lead to unnecessary stress as we fixate on outcomes that may never occur. Similarly, we might worry about health issues or accidents that have no basis in reality, yet our minds still become consumed with these fears. These exaggerated worries can distract us from addressing the immediate, more relevant issues in our lives.

How can we clearly understand fear in the first place?

We don't fear looking at heights, but we fear what might happen if we fall.

We don't fear darkness, but we fear what could be hidden in that darkness.

We don't fear love, but we fear the conflicts and separations that might come with it.

We don't fear death itself, but we fear what might happen in life before it comes.

We don't fear the people around us, but we fear that they might reject us.

We don't fear our circumstances, but we fear accepting the truth.

We don't fear making an effort, but we fear what to do if our efforts fail.

We don't fear speaking in a group, but we fear being misunderstood.

We don't fear losing a job, but we fear the impact on food and family circumstances.

We don't fear animals, but we fear their aggressive actions.

We don't fear driving fast, but we fear what might happen if we crash.

We don't fear exams, but we fear being judged poorly.

Fear is an emotion within us. We cannot completely eliminate it, but we can understand it and learn to control it.

How else can we manage fear?

Fear is, in a way, an illusion as well. Fear arises because we are not truly living in the present moment; instead, we are trapped in our minds. Fear is always tied to what might happen next, which means it is about something that doesn't exist. If our fear revolves around the non-existent, it is entirely imaginary. Suffering over something imaginary can be considered a form of insanity. While society may accept certain levels of this as normal, being afraid or suffering over what doesn't exist is still, essentially, irrational.

We often dwell on what happened yesterday or worry about what might happen tomorrow, which means we are suffering over things that don't exist. This happens because we are not grounded in reality but are caught up in our minds. The mind consists of two aspects: memory and imagination. Both are forms of imagination because neither exists in the present moment.

This tendency to get lost in imagination is the root of fear. However, if we anchor ourselves in reality, we can overcome and manage fear effectively.

Fear can be described as "False Evidence Appearing Real." Often, there is no genuine threat of immediate physical danger, no risk of losing someone or something valuable, and, in reality, nothing to fear at all. Fear is an illusion—a creation of our minds that we convince ourselves is real.

As you are in love with a woman, but you have a fear in your heart that she is getting closer to someone else, the real fear is not about her but about your love for her. How can this be managed? Fear prevents us from growing. If you let fear take hold of your love, how will you take it to the next level?

First, understand your beloved. The loss caused by fear is something you alone will bear. Don't let fear diminish the depth of your love, as it might eventually lead to her feeling distant or even resentful toward you.

When expressing love, there is the fear that she might not accept you. If she accepts you, there is the fear that she might one day leave you. This cycle of fear can hinder your ability to experience and nurture true love.

Think of your fear as a lie. If you think, "I acted out of fear," remind yourself that nothing will happen beyond that. If fear becomes overwhelming, and you believe it will lead to something happening, reflect on what you can do about it. Fear will not write the end of your story. It is merely a thought. If we focus on a non-existent fear, we shrink our lives and diminish our true potential.

When we experience fear, it often comes from our imagination. For example:

When we go to the beach, we imagine what might happen if we face strong waves.

When we stand on a slope, we imagine what it would feel like if we fell from above.

When we walk on a wooden bridge, we imagine what it would be like if we stumbled and fell.

When we sail on a boat in the sea, we imagine how the boat would rock if the storm comes.

When we ride a train, we fear what might happen if another train crashes into us.

When the earth shakes, we fear how things would look if it worsens.

These fears arise when we imagine possible scenarios. The moment we start imagining, fear takes hold. To overcome this, we must work to clear our imaginations and take action in the present. By doing so, managing fear becomes much easier.

ॐॐॐ

FOUR

THE PERCEPTION OF ANGER

What is Anger? Sadness, something that humans cannot avoid or easily resolve, often turns into anger. Anger is an emotion that all humans experience in similar ways. But why do we feel anger toward others? What causes it? Sometimes, when we realize that those close to us are not who we thought they were, anger builds up inside us. In relationships, when we find that a person is not what we expected or hoped for, anger naturally follows.

However, there is no need for them to be as we expect them to be. Just like how we might not expect them to be what we hope for, we also don't think about whether we are the ones they expect. That expectation, which we place within ourselves, is what creates discomfort. And in that moment, doesn't it seem like there's no benefit in getting angry?

Anger, as an emotion, possesses the extraordinary power to disrupt lives, often leaving long-lasting effects. Consider Gokul, a young man from Chennai who worked at an egg shop. One day, while carrying eggs for delivery, he tripped and fell, breaking every egg he had. In that moment, his physical pain from the fall was overshadowed by an even greater fear: How would he explain the situation to his boss? He worried not only about the monetary loss but also about the potential consequences for his job and his family's financial security.

In this scenario, the perspective of the manager becomes crucial. Had the manager reacted angrily, it could have cost Gokul his job, putting his family under immense strain. However, the story takes a surprising turn those who witnessed the incident contributed a collective amount that exceeded the value of the broken eggs. This highlights a vital truth: How we respond to a situation not only affects the immediate outcome but also defines the ripple effects it has on those involved. A calm and understanding approach can transform what might seem like a disaster into an opportunity for kindness and connection.

Similarly, in our daily lives, we often allow anger to take precedence over reason, especially in fleeting moments. For instance, when we're in a cab and cross paths with someone on the road, we may snap at them without considering their age, situation, or the circumstances. This impulsive reaction might ruin their day and create unnecessary animosity. Moreover, we rarely stop to reflect on our own potential mistakes in such scenarios.

Imagine if, instead of lashing out, we chose to calmly say, "Sorry, I wasn't paying attention to the right of way." A simple apology could diffuse the tension, leaving the other person with a smile. Later, they might even reflect on the incident, questioning if they were truly at fault. This shift in response not only avoids conflict but also fosters introspection and mutual understanding.

However, failing to approach such situations thoughtfully can have unintended consequences. By acting out in anger, we might unknowingly instill feelings of self-doubt or inferiority in the other person. While it may seem trivial at the moment, these interactions can compound over time, subtly influencing someone's confidence and self-perception.

Ultimately, the way we handle our anger and our interactions with others holds the power to either harm or heal. It's a choice that defines not only the impact of a single moment but also the tone of our broader relationships and experiences.

Humans have developed an uncanny ability to react quickly to negativity. When someone makes a mistake, our first instinct is often to criticize or reprimand them without stopping to assess whether their error was intentional or even significant. We tend to prioritize reacting over understanding, and this impulsivity has become a defining characteristic of how we handle situations. Quick fixes often driven by anger have become a societal norm, but they frequently lead to unresolved issues and lingering bitterness.

Anger, when left unchecked, tends to manifest in negative ways. It turns fleeting frustrations into long-lasting resentment. Ironically, while we are quick to advise others on managing their emotions, we often fail to apply the same wisdom to ourselves. We fall prey to the same cycle of unjustified anger, which not only harms us but also deeply affects those around us, creating ripples that influence our personal relationships, workplace dynamics, and overall environment.

Consider simple, everyday scenarios: when we visit a hotel and our food takes a few extra minutes to arrive, we get upset. Our frustration over such trivial delays stems from a misguided belief that expressing anger asserts our importance or authority. What we fail to recognize is how this behaviour negatively impacts the people around us, creating a hostile and uncomfortable atmosphere. Similarly, when we try to cross the road and a car interrupts us, we instinctively blame the driver. Yet, is it fair to channel our frustration at them, especially when we might have been crossing at the wrong time or place?

The irony is glaring when we reverse roles. If we are driving on the wrong side of the road and someone blocks our path, we still find a way to direct our anger outward, refusing to acknowledge our own mistake. Similarly, when stuck in traffic, we vent at others without recognizing that we, too, contribute to the congestion. This lack of introspection perpetuates a cycle of misplaced anger and missed accountability.

On a deeper level, our interactions and relationships also suffer from our inability to manage anger constructively. We often expect others to agree with us, and when they don't, disagreements escalate into arguments. In these moments, we rarely consider that differing perspectives are natural and healthy. Instead, we let anger dictate the situation. Similarly, when someone shares a negative opinion about someone else, we tend to get upset with the person being criticized, rarely pausing to question the validity of the claims. Even if that individual has done good for us in the past, their positive actions are often overshadowed by our misplaced anger.

Stress and exhaustion exacerbate this tendency. When overwhelmed, we redirect our frustrations toward those closest to us, often without reason. This irritation-based anger stems not from logic but from emotional exhaustion. For instance, when someone criticizes our favourite actor or actress on social media, we jump into the comments section, argue, and fuel an unnecessary conflict. In that moment, defending our preference seems like the most important thing in our lives. Similarly, in professional settings, if a manager micromanages us, we quickly interpret it as a lack of trust rather than an effort to guide or support us. This perceived threat turns into frustration and anger, further straining workplace relationships.

The consequences of anger are significant. It creates hardships not just for us but also for those around us. That's why it's crucial for our anger to be justified and grounded in genuine reasons. Taking offense at someone who points out our flaws is counterproductive, especially when their perception may not align with reality. However, the deeper issue lies in attributing self-loathing or insecurities to anger, which often distorts our responses and creates more harm than good.

At times, even understanding can become dangerous if it leads to overthinking or impulsive actions. Anger has a way of clouding judgment, preventing us from thinking clearly and making rational decisions. It rushes us into reactions that we later regret, overshadowing the opportunities for growth, connection, and resolution that lie in front of us.

In managing anger, the focus should not only be on control but also on understanding its origins. Why do we get angry? Is our anger justified or simply a projection of internal struggles? Answering these questions with honesty and introspection allows us to transform anger from a destructive force into an opportunity for self-awareness and improvement.

Anger can sometimes be triggered by changes in the environment, such as the heat during a sunny day, which may cause irritation that manifests as anger toward others. In such moments, the words we speak or the decisions we make may turn out to be wrong. Anger often blinds us to the good opportunities ahead. For example, if you're an athlete and experience disappointment over a lack of time or poor performance, that sadness can transform into anger, disrupting your focus. However, successful athletes demonstrate the ability to remain focused and undistracted, no matter the circumstances.

"Losers always focus on winners, but winners always focus on winning."

This is also applicable to our lives.

When managed carefully, anger can sometimes pave the way to success. Anger itself isn't always bad. Interestingly, many motivational speakers focus on how to control anger but often overlook explaining why it arises in the first place. Even on platforms like YouTube or Instagram, the emphasis is on controlling anger rather than understanding its root cause. Take a moment to pause and reflect on why we feel angry, and whether that anger is justified or counterproductive. If the reason isn't clear, revisit this discussion from the beginning, and you'll gain better insight into the origins of your anger.

ᗡᗡᗡ

FIVE

THE PERCEPTION OF BLISS

There are two kinds of happiness in life: the happiness we are aware of and the happiness we remain unaware of. Happiness is as essential to human existence as food; just as our bodies grow weary without nourishment, our spirits become fatigued without moments of joy in our lives.

Do you know what the happiness we don't recognize looks like?

In a world filled with jealousy and competition, happiness often emerges in simple, unexpected moments.

It's the joy we feel when we see children, untouched by envy or rivalry, just being themselves.

It's the small delight of giving a thumbs-up to someone who lets us pass on the road while traveling.

It's the surprise happiness that lights up our day when a girlfriend or boyfriend gives a gift at an unexpected moment.

In the morning rush to the office, happiness sneaks in when we receive an unanticipated email saying the manager is on leave.

It's the quiet joy of gazing at the evening sky when we are alone, lost in thought.

There's even a strange sense of amusement when two people argue or scuffle on the road. Reality shows like Bigg Boss thrive on tapping into this peculiar sense of satisfaction.

Then, there's the relief of stepping into the comfort of home after wandering around under the blazing sun.

These moments of happiness are unplanned and spontaneous, but they hold a charm we cannot ignore or resist.

Our experience of happiness depends largely on our perspective. For instance, we believe that starting the day by listening to a motivational video or song sets a positive tone for the entire day.

Getting motivated by external sources is not permanent; motivating yourself is a lasting solution.
This shows that we don't need to waste time searching for motivation elsewhere it's something we can cultivate within ourselves.

We often feel joy when events align perfectly with what our minds anticipate. Now, don't let anger cloud your thoughts just hear me out. The truth is, happiness doesn't always need a reason. How happy we feel often depends on how we perceive and compare our actions with those of others. But what drives the happiness we experience when helping others?

Why is helping others so fulfilling?

Helping others is, in many ways, helping ourselves. This simple yet profound truth reflects the interconnectedness of our lives. Consider the joy we feel watching children selflessly help those around them—it's pure and heartwarming. But how often do we forget that we once possessed that same selflessness as children? Over time, as we grow and adapt to societal norms, we are subtly taught to prioritize personal gain, often at the expense of compassion and generosity. This shift is a bitter reality, influenced by the very systems and education that shape our adult lives.

When we extend a helping hand to others, it's not just their lives that improve. Our own lives are enriched in ways we may not immediately realize. Helping others reduces stress, enhances mental health, and brings a profound sense of fulfillment. It's a unique joy, akin to the satisfaction of achieving something meaningful. Yet, while helping others is undeniably rewarding, we must also focus on nurturing our own happiness. Striving for contentment in life—regardless of whether things go as planned—builds resilience. It equips us with the strength and confidence to face life's inevitable uncertainties. Happiness is, at its core, a choice. And when we pause to reflect, we can see just how pivotal this choice is to our well-being.

A common misconception is that happiness stems from wealth or status. Many aspire to the lives of individuals like Bill Gates or Elon Musk, equating their success with ultimate happiness. But this view oversimplifies the complexity of life. First, we must understand that not everyone can—or should—aspire to be billionaires. If everyone became a Bill Gates or an Elon Musk, who would play the essential roles that sustain society? True success is not measured by wealth alone; it is about perspective, balance, and understanding. We must learn to admire the achievements of iconic figures while also valuing the seemingly ordinary but equally important lives of those around us, such as our neighbors.

Happiness is not inherently tied to the amount of money in our bank accounts. It is a state of mind that flows from having enough to meet our needs and cherishing what we already have. Ironically, those who relentlessly chase wealth often find little time to enjoy the fruits of their labor. Instead, their loved ones may be the ones reaping the benefits. Consider the lives of the children of the wealthy and successful—like Jennifer Gates, Anant Ambani, Preston Bezos, or Cristiano Ronaldo's son, Angel. While they may enjoy privileged lifestyles, their parents, often consumed by work, may not always get the chance to savor those moments alongside them.

Ultimately, equating happiness solely with financial success risks depriving us of the deeper joys of life. True happiness lies in striking a balance—earning enough to support our needs while making time to appreciate and share the moments that truly matter. When we focus on kindness, gratitude, and connection, we discover that happiness isn't something we chase—it's something we create.

While others may lack the mindset of contentment, do you, as a reader of this book, possess it? For someone riding a two-wheeler, a thousand rupees might feel like a fortune, while for someone in a four-wheeler, it might take a hundred thousand rupees to evoke the same feeling. Instead of focusing on preserving and appreciating what we already have, we often fixate on the pursuit of earning more.

Money plays a crucial role in our lives, but it alone cannot bring us true happiness. Why is it that even nature lovers sometimes fail to find joy in the simple wonders of nature? When will we realize that we, too, are a part of nature? We are interconnected with it, and happiness is an inherent aspect of that connection.

Happiness cannot be measured by material possessions or external factors. Nothing in this world is permanent—not even the world itself. We, like specks of dust, carry an incredible depth of emotion within us. The key lies in focusing on the power of our thoughts.

Our brains are incredibly powerful, and what we think shapes who we become. We don't always need external advice; our minds are capable of guiding us. The unique ability of the brain is that it can control itself—we can choose what thoughts to embrace and which to let go of. Harnessing this power allows us to shape our experiences and find true fulfilment.

SIX

THE PERCEPTION OF DEPENDENCY

We often hear people say, "Don't depend on anyone." But is that really true?

Do we ever need someone's help or favour?

The reality is that everything in this world is, in one way or another, interconnected and dependent on others.

Everyone says that dependency in life is a myth, but they fail to understand that dependency is an integral part of life.

Dependency is a natural part of life, but it's important to understand it in the right way. Many on social media claim that to be happy, you shouldn't depend on anyone, yet this mindset can mislead us. Ironically, those who make such claims are themselves dependent on their audience and viewers. Funny!

If matter and antimatter had not been dependent on each other, this universe would not have been formed.

We often say the sky rejoices when it rains, but we fail to recognize that rain falls from the sky because the Earth is burdened by its own turmoil.

If the Earth didn't rely on its gravitational pull, the planets as we know them wouldn't exist.

Animals depend on food, humans depend on money, and people often rely on those who have it. Christianity depends on their Bible, and the cycle of dependence continues to build in various forms.

In some way or another, we all depend on someone. At birth, we rely on our parents; in school, on our teachers; at work, on our managers; after marriage, on our families; and in times of illness, on doctors. Dependence is a form of trust.

It's those who have lost faith in life who believe we should never depend on anyone.

If we truly believed we weren't dependent on the driver while riding, we would never take the ride. Just as one atom relies on another to form everything around us, we too are inherently interconnected. Yet, with our knowledge, we've managed to convince ourselves that we are separate. This isn't a flaw—it's simply the nature of things.

What matters is discerning what to depend on and what not to. The irony is that while some tell us not to depend on others for happiness, they believe money is essential for that happiness and ultimately rely on others to earn it. If you work in an office, you depend on your manager; if you're a businessperson, you depend on your customers. Dependence is unavoidable; it's how we navigate it that defines our experience.

Whether it's a motivational speaker or close friends advising us not to depend on others to avoid getting hurt, is that truly the reason? In reality, your dependence on others often stems from your emotions.

There is a saying "Expectations are not always fulfilling our life". As here said, When things don't go as planned, it's natural to feel a sense of disappointment or despair. In those moments, we often let our emotions spiral into thoughts of hopelessness, believing that similar opportunities or outcomes are forever lost. But when we ask ourselves who bears the responsibility for such feelings—is it the fault of others or our own reaction—the answer often lies within us.

To cope, many of us turn to the belief that if God hasn't granted what we hoped for, it must be because something better awaits. This comforting thought allows us to move forward with faith. But a critical question arises: why do we readily extend such understanding to a divine figure, yet struggle to do the same for the people in our lives? If we applied the same grace and trust to our relationships, we might see a profound shift in our emotional landscape.

Consider this: when we argue with our spouse, quarrel with a partner, or fall out with a friend, these conflicts often stem from unmet expectations or a lack of understanding. If we were to trust these individuals with the same faith we reserve for an unseen deity, we might approach these situations with greater patience and empathy. By doing so, we would reduce misunderstandings, mend relationships more quickly, and ease the emotional burdens we carry.

The irony here is striking. We trust an invisible figure like God, someone intangible, beyond sight or touch, with our deepest fears and desires. Yet, we hesitate to place that same trust in the very people who surround us—those who can physically stand by us, offer support, and share our burdens. Why? Perhaps it's because speaking to an unseen presence feels safer; there's no fear of rejection, criticism, or misunderstanding. This dynamic makes it easier to pour out our feelings without restraint.

However, when we "share our stress" with God, what we're often doing is engaging in a form of self-soothing. We're advising ourselves, reframing our thoughts, and finding ways to console our hearts. It's a dialogue within, cloaked in the belief that we're communicating with something greater. And while this process is valuable, it also highlights a truth we sometimes overlook: we are deeply interdependent creatures.

No man or woman can exist in complete isolation. Human connection is woven into the very fabric of life. Our existence thrives on relationships, support, and shared experiences. Dependence isn't a weakness; it's a fundamental aspect of being human. The sooner we embrace this reality, the more harmonious and fulfilling our lives can become. By trusting and understanding others as much as we strive to trust in the unseen, we not only strengthen our relationships but also enrich our own sense of purpose and belonging.

We readily accept unexpected gifts or events, but we struggle to accept when the things we anticipate don't materialize. Life is like a metamorphosis, if we don't rely on the next stage and take the necessary steps, we risk stagnating in our current phase. It's through dependence that we truly come to understand ourselves.

A politician should depend on the people they serve, not on the politics they navigate. Similarly, a salesperson should focus on building trust with customers, not just on chasing money—when the focus is right, the money will follow naturally. Ultimately, our lives are shaped by our thoughts, not merely by the events that unfold around us.

Primitive humans relied on one another, and it is this interdependence that gave rise to what we now call society. It's also the reason we are able to read this book today.

Aren't Christians dependent on Jesus? Don't Muslims rely on Allah? Don't Hindus look to the Bhagavad Gita for guidance? Take a moment to reflect—God, in essence, often represents nature itself. Whether it's Allah, the Fire God, the Sun God, or Yahweh, all these figures symbolize the greater forces that govern existence.

So, in truth, do we depend on nature under the name of God? The marvel of nature and the profound thoughts it inspires are nothing short of breathtaking.

ᗡᗡᗡ

SEVEN

THE PERCEPTION OF LIFE WITH TIME OR TIME WITH LIFE

Is our journey through life, or is it through time? This is often a point of confusion. The bitter truth is that while we move forward in life, its meaning often unravels only when we look back.

Consider this: clock-watchers merely try, minute-watchers progress, but those who focus on the seconds truly succeed. Time flies faster than we realize, and in its haste, we've forgotten pivotal cases—Ramkumar Swati from Chennai, Asifa from Kashmir, and Nirbhaya from Delhi. Why? Because we're always ready to share the next trending event or case on social media.

In today's world, all media craves attention. When someone captures the spotlight, they often gain popularity. Surprise! Do we really have so much time to spare, or is that person more important than our time itself?

If we didn't spend time criticizing or supporting others unnecessarily, many undeserving individuals wouldn't gain popularity. This, in turn, would preserve the distinction between true talent and mediocrity. What the media demands is our attention, and what our attention demands is our time. It's a cycle that constantly drains the precious seconds we could otherwise use to shape our own journey.

Time can be likened to our emotions—a master illusionist. It drags when we wait, mirrors our feelings when we're sad, and seems to vanish when we're happy. When we're nervous, time feels stagnant, almost as if it's paused. Time behaves like our thoughts, and our thoughts are shaped by our perspective.

Why do we place so much value on time? Do we believe that time passes on its own, or do we perceive it as simply flowing by? The truth is, we've learned to navigate and even outwit time in our journey—a testament to our resilience and growth.

Have you ever wondered why we often fail to celebrate geniuses during their lifetimes? Nikola Tesla, who gave us the radio and the wireless electricity transformer, was never truly celebrated while he was alive. Charles Darwin revolutionized our understanding of life's evolution, yet his ideas were largely dismissed during his time. Albert Einstein's theory of black holes was met with skepticism, and he was viewed more as an eccentric innovator than a genius.

Patience plays a crucial role in this dynamic. Just as a leaf falls from a tree in the wind but grows back with time and resilience, our lives follow a similar rhythm. It's through time and faith that we rebuild and flourish.

Life and time reveal their true beauty when we shift our perspective, viewing our journey from a broader, more reflective angle. Only then can we appreciate the intricate interplay of challenges and triumphs that shape our path.

What do you think? Am I motivating you? Of course not!

Buddha once said: "Your biggest mistake is thinking you have time."

Time is free, yet it's priceless. You can't own it, but you can use it. You can't save it, but you can spend it. And once it's gone, you can never get it back.

The average person lives 78 years. Out of that, we spend 28.3 years sleeping—almost one-third of our life—yet 30% of people struggle with sleep. Ironically funny, isn't it? We spend 10.5 years working, but over half of us wish to leave our current jobs.

People often say, "Time is more valuable than money," and it couldn't be truer. You can earn more money, but you can't earn more time. Consider this: we spend 9 years watching TV and scrolling social media, 6 years doing chores, 4 years eating and drinking, 3.5 years in education, 2.5 years grooming, 2.5 years shopping, 1.5 years caring for children, and 1.3 years commuting.

When all is said and done, we're left with just 9 years of free time.

The question is: how will you choose to spend those precious years?

Steve Jobs once said, "Your time is limited, so don't waste it living someone else's life." There's both good news and bad news about time. The bad news is that it flies, but the good news? You're the pilot.

Now, imagine this: your father has 2.5 billion rupees and deposits 86,400 rupees into your bank account every single day. You spend all of it daily, and the next day, he deposits another 86,400 rupees. This continues for 28,429.5 days—the equivalent of 2.5 billion rupees.

At the end of it all, he asks, "What have you gained from the 2.5 billion?" If your answer is "Nothing," then you've merely managed to get by.

This is a metaphor for time—every day, you're given 86,400 seconds. What will you do with them? Will you use them wisely or let them slip away without a return?

The choice is yours: will you turn 2.5 billion into 5 billion, or let it dwindle to zero?

Always remember, it's not about how much time we have but how we choose to use it. Each day gives us 86,400 seconds—how will you make the most of them?

To understand the value of a year, ask a student who failed a grade.

To grasp the value of a month, ask a mother who lost her child in the final month of pregnancy.

To appreciate the value of a week, ask the editor of an online magazine racing against deadlines.

To recognize the value of an hour, ask a couple in a long-distance relationship cherishing their rare moments together.

To feel the weight of a minute, ask someone who just missed a bus, train, or plane.

To comprehend the value of a second, ask someone who narrowly avoided an accident or won Olympic gold.

And to truly understand the value of a millisecond, ask the athlete who came second at the Olympics.

We often think others are wasting our time, but in truth, we're the ones allowing it to happen. In reality, these dynamics exist within us.

Never let someone be a priority when you're merely an option to them. Some of us lose the most important people in our lives because we fail to value their time. Others don't realize someone's significance until they're no longer around.

Within each of us are two voices. One voice encourages us to rise, while the other holds us back. One voice pushes us to grow, and the other tempts us to remain stagnant. One voice drives us to act, while the other lulls us into complacency. That second voice—the one that restricts us—stands between us and our full potential. Recognizing which voice to follow makes all the difference.

Every day, from the moment we wake up to the moment we fall asleep, an inner battle takes place between two voices. And which one wins? The one we listen to the most, the one we nurture, the one we amplify. Ultimately, it's our choice how we use our time and which voice we allow to guide us.

Life and time are our greatest teachers. Life shows us how to make the best use of time, while time reveals the true value of life.

William Shakespeare beautifully said:

"Time is very slow for those who wait,

very fast for those who fear,

very long for those who grieve,

and very short for those who rejoice.

But for those who love, time is eternal."

We often reflect on the past to understand the significance of time in this world. But why do we always say that success in life is essential, no matter who we admire? Why do we frequently cite wealthy individuals like Warren Buffett or Ambani as examples? Are they all college graduates?

Wait a minute!

Those reading this book might instantly think, "It's crucial to go to school." But why does this thought arise so quickly? Why don't we immediately consider educated geniuses like Sundar Pichai, Mark Zuckerberg, Elon Musk, Warren Buffett, or Bill Gates? After all, they are graduates.

Our brain processes information based on how our mind perceives it. Just as we cannot always assume that what we think now is correct, we cannot assume it's always wrong either. Our thoughts are shaped by perspective and context.

Time is like a river—you can never touch the same water twice because the flow that has passed will never return. Cherish every moment of your life. Time feels slow when you're waiting and fast when you're running late. Every experience with time is shaped by your emotions and psychological state, not by the ticking of a clock. So, make the most of your time and create meaningful moments with others.

Pardon me! I am not going to say that.

What would you obey if I told you? The choice is yours. It's in your hands to decide which path to take and which to avoid. While time feels significant to us here, we drift into another world when we sleep. No matter how often I admire the wonders of nature, it never feels sufficient. Take a moment to realize just how valuable time truly is.

ϷϷϷ

EIGHT

THE PERCEPTION OF RELATIONSHIP

When we think about the topic of relationships, the first thing that usually comes to mind is the relationship between a man and a woman. This is a common and widely accepted notion. However, love is not limited to this. It exists between a brother and a sister, between a child and their parents, and even between a student and a teacher. Love extends to our bond with animals as well. Over time, we have mistakenly narrowed the concept of love to just the romantic relationship between a man and a woman. Now, we are going to explore and challenge that misunderstanding.

Who truly experiences love these days? Many argue that genuine love has become rare. Today, it seems that many people only "love" when it serves their needs. However, love is not merely a relationship—relationships involve something else entirely. Love is the willingness to be with a romantic partner, a mutual commitment between two people. It uplifts you and brings a sense of fulfilment.

Love can inspire, but it can also be influenced by certain qualities that captivate the mind. It could be someone's physical appearance, the alignment of their emotional nature with your subconscious thoughts, their way of speaking, their actions, or how they interact with you. Love is what you create and build together. However, when an unbearable situation arises, that fragile bond can break, and love may falter.

We often think of love as something external, like air, and begin searching for it outside ourselves. But love is something that originates within the mind. Emotions such as happiness, hatred, sorrow, anger, or conflict do not come from external sources—they are internal, born from within us.

We describe love as a feeling, but is it truly a feeling, or is it a decision? Decisions are typically made when something aligns with our interests, and love often follows the same principle. Before committing to love, we evaluate whether it benefits us in some way. However, when we realize that the relationship no longer serves our interests, love can break.

At times, we cling to the decisions we've made, fearing the consequences of admitting they were wrong. Those who understand the selfless nature of love are more likely to preserve it. On the other hand, for those who misinterpret or misunderstand this nature, love often transforms into resentment.

This resentment can lead to anger, which then becomes a justification for seeking another relationship or withdrawing entirely. In fear of repeating past mistakes, we may choose isolation instead of taking the risk of loving again.

Are you trying to control your partner in a relationship? If so, that's a serious mistake. For instance, some men try to dictate how women should dress or what they should wear, believing they need to prevent others from forming inappropriate opinions. This mindset is flawed. After entering a relationship, men often feel a sense of ownership over their partner and worry about how others might perceive them. However, imposing restrictions on a woman's clothing infringes on her freedom and autonomy.

Such behavior can lead to the first cracks in a relationship. It's important to understand that we cannot control how others think or behave, nor can we dictate how they view someone. By fixating on these concerns and acting out of fear based on imagined scenarios, you risk damaging your relationship. Trust and mutual respect are key, and any attempt to control or limit your partner's choices undermines these foundations.

Forbidding your partner from interacting with others, especially from talking to friends of the opposite sex, is an unhealthy practice. Attempting to control whom someone communicates with is a significant mistake and often becomes the root cause of relationship breakdowns. Such restrictions can create misunderstandings and resentment in your partner's mind.

Human nature tends to resist being told what not to do. When restrictions are imposed, they often lead to the opposite outcome, as people naturally rebel against such limitations. This behaviour is not unique to either men or women—it's simply how humans respond to control.

Imposing these boundaries does nothing to change the underlying fears in your mind. Instead, it can drive your partner to seek the freedom and kindness they feel you're denying them in others. This can eventually lead to the deterioration of your relationship and the possibility of your partner finding emotional connection elsewhere.

The key to a healthy relationship is trust and mutual respect. Attempting to control your partner only fuels insecurity and pushes them away, jeopardizing the bond you share.

Women's love often grows out of their needs and family circumstances. However, such love may not always endure. In some instances, men bear responsibility for this. While men may put significant effort into winning love, they often fail to invest the same energy in maintaining and nurturing it over time.

Love is not a destination; it is a progress!

When some women lack the care and attention they receive at home, they may become vulnerable to men who use enticing words to lure them into love. These men, driven by selfish desires, pursue the relationship for personal pleasure and later end it, leaving the woman emotionally hurt. This experience often leaves the woman fearful of love. Exploiting someone's emotions for personal gain is a deeply harmful and irreparable mistake.

Social media has become a significant factor in relationships today, often contributing to misunderstandings and even preventing love from leading to marriage. One common issue is the unrealistic expectation for men or women to emulate the idealized personas seen on social media. When we adopt such mindsets, we inadvertently set the stage for relationship failure.

The qualities and perspectives you initially admire in your partner should remain consistent throughout the relationship. If change is desired, it's important to discuss it openly, explaining why the change is necessary and exploring possible alternatives together.

Men and women often approach problems differently—men might focus on anticipating their partner's reaction, while women tend to analyse the issue from various angles and assumptions. However, these differences can be navigated by clearly communicating expectations. Is it fair to expect something from your partner without expressing those expectations? Openly sharing thoughts and desires can prevent many conflicts and foster a deeper understanding between partners.

Is understanding love only possible after experiencing heartbreak? Why do many believe that someone who has faced failure in love is better equipped to understand it? Some argue that it's entirely possible to comprehend love deeply even in a lasting first relationship. Why should someone need to experience loss to understand the essence of love?

These days, many claim to fall in love during their school years. This is often attributed to youthful impulsiveness. At that stage, we rarely consider the bigger picture of our future or our life goals. During moments of aimlessness, our minds can easily fixate on the idea of love.

Parents play a crucial role in guiding young minds in such situations. When they impose strict restrictions like forbidding their children from talking to the opposite gender, using phones for chats, or socializing freely, it often leads to curiosity about what's being prohibited. When children break these rules, they often feel hesitant to confide in their parents and end up hiding their actions.

Instead of creating barriers, parents should foster open communication by addressing the consequences of certain behaviours in a friendly, nonjudgmental way. Treating children as equals in conversations builds trust and encourages them to share their thoughts and experiences openly, creating a healthier and more supportive relationship.

Don't compare your relationship to others. Thinking, "They do this, so we should do that too; they bought a car, so we should get one; he goes to the gym and has a six-pack, so you should get one too, and then I can post about it on Instagram; he treats his girlfriend a certain way and buys her everything she wants, so you should do the same" is a flawed mindset.

Love that is based solely on physical appearance or material gestures doesn't last. Physical traits and beauty are temporary and subject to change, but the one thing that remains constant is a person's character and mindset. Trying to force someone to change or waiting for them to become what you desire only leads to frustration, jealousy, and conflict. True love thrives on acceptance, understanding, and appreciating your partner for who they are, not by comparing them to others.

Don't seek and give the Expectation.

Expectations—or the act of giving without clear communication—are often the root cause of many relationship breakups today. Some believe that love means your partner should automatically understand your unspoken expectations, but that's far from true. Neither men nor women are mind readers capable of knowing what the other is thinking.

It's not about avoiding expectations altogether; rather, it's about asking: How will the other person know what you need if you don't express it? Why not take the time to communicate and try to understand each other instead? Open dialogue about your expectations can prevent misunderstandings and strengthen your bond.

Men and women often make promises to their partners with ease: I'll come to see you at this time, or I'll take you here and definitely buy this for you. However, when work or other circumstances prevent them from fulfilling these promises, it can lead to significant disappointment for their partner.

A promise becomes an expectation for the other person, and that expectation turns into hope. When that hope is repeatedly broken, it breeds confusion and doubt in the relationship. This confusion can lead to fear—fear of the relationship failing—which may escalate into anger over even minor issues. That anger can ultimately result in the end of the relationship.

Before making a promise, take a moment to think carefully: Can I truly follow through on this? A thoughtful commitment is far better than one made hastily, only to be broken later.

In any relationship, there is often one dominant person—it's a natural dynamic. Similarly, one partner may talk more while the other tends to listen. A lack of time spent together is often the root cause of many relationship issues. Love and relationships are not without their challenges, but ignoring problems will only allow them to grow.

When an issue arises, the solution lies in both partners sitting down to communicate openly. Even if it leads to a work-related disagreement, addressing the problem is far better than avoiding it altogether. Avoidance only creates tension and distance.

When we sought the relationship initially, we made time for it. Why then, after being in the relationship, do we claim we have no time? The truth is, everyone has time—they just need the willingness to prioritize it. Instead of checking social media, use that time to connect with your partner.

For instance, women often find comfort in being heard. They don't always expect solutions to their concerns—sometimes, they just want someone to listen. Show support by lending an ear and offering a few comforting words. Avoid trying to "fix" everything, as that may not always be what they need.

Many family arguments and misunderstandings could be avoided if both partners set aside time to talk and truly listen to each other. Think about it!

Don't Carry your Emotional baggage into your relationship from your past one!

If you were cheated on in a previous relationship, it's unfair to carry that fear into your current one. Assuming your current partner will act the same way or imposing restrictions—such as forbidding them from going out with friends or talking to certain people—will not only harm your current relationship but could jeopardize any future ones as well.

Women often carry unresolved issues from past fights into new arguments with their partner, letting emotional baggage from the past resurface. This can diminish the true significance of the current disagreement. Men are also guilty of making the same mistake.

Carrying emotional baggage into a relationship can cloud judgment and create unnecessary conflict. The key is to address and resolve past issues so they don't influence your present. This principle doesn't just apply to relationships—it's equally important in life and in the workplace. Let go of the past to avoid letting it dictate your future.

ppp

NINE

THE PERCEPTION OF VALUE

Why is it that some people, despite having skills and physical strength, struggle to earn money, while others can earn without needing physical effort? The wealthy often claim that money doesn't bring happiness, while those who are less fortunate believe that money can solve all their problems. In truth, money has the power to reveal who we truly are.

What is humanity's greatest invention? Could it be fire, providing warmth, protection, and the means to cook our food? Or perhaps the wheel, the foundation of trade, commerce, and travel? While both are remarkable choices, we often overlook one of the most significant inventions of all: money.

Unlike other great inventions, money is intangible. This may be why we rarely regard it with the same reverence as fire or the wheel. Tangible creations like fire and the wheel have a physical presence, while money is an abstract concept—an illusion whose value exists only because we collectively assign importance to it. At least, that's the case with money as we know it today.

However, its intangible nature does not diminish its significance. On the contrary, the fact that money is an idea underscores its profound impact on shaping human society.

Before money existed, we relied on the barter system, where goods and services were exchanged directly for other goods and services. In this system, value wasn't fixed but determined by what each party was willing to trade. It was almost like a game—if I wanted your vegetables for dinner but only raised cattle, I'd have to trade you one of my animals for a few bags of vegetables. Similarly, if I needed shoes but made tents, I might have to give up an entire tent for a single pair of slippers.

This system, however, had a glaring issue: asymmetry. For instance, as a tent maker, trading a whole living space for simple footwear would likely feel unfair. Without a standardized medium of exchange, it was incredibly challenging to find two people whose needs perfectly aligned. This inefficiency, known as the "double coincidence of wants," made trade cumbersome and time-consuming.

But the problems didn't stop there. Money isn't just a medium of exchange; it's also a store of value. Before its invention, many people were unable to preserve their wealth, not due to a lack of effort, but because of the nature of their goods. Take, for example, a farmer who grows tomatoes and a tent maker. The tent maker could create an entire village of shelters and barter them year-round with anyone needing a place to stay, likely accumulating substantial wealth.

In contrast, the tomato farmer faced limitations. Tomatoes are perishable, and he could only trade during the harvest season. He had no means to store his wealth beyond that period, even though his effort matched that of the tent maker. This inherent imbalance made it nearly impossible for certain individuals to achieve lasting wealth under the barter system.

There is also the problem of having something that only few people want. Nowadays, when starting a business, you are often told to find a niche. A small group of people who are very interested in what you have to offer. Before money was a thing, that advice would have left you with nothing worth bartering. The people who had the most were those who owned things that everybody wanted. Things, weapon, animal skin, and salt. But then since everyone know that everyone wanted these things, they started buying them even if they did not need them at the time just so they could trade with them later. And so, commodity money became a thing.

People began exchanging goods and services for universally desired items like salt or weapons, which they could then trade for something they actually needed. Over time, these items expanded to include smaller objects like shells and beads, marking a significant advancement in trade. Instead of directly bartering goods and services for other goods and services you might not need immediately, people could trade for arbitrary objects that served as placeholders of value—essentially an IOU (I Owe You). These placeholders could then be exchanged later for items or services they genuinely wanted.

The concept was ingenious, so much so that it gradually led to the decline of the barter system and the rise of money-based trade. However, this new medium of exchange came with its own challenge. For money to hold value, it needs to be scarce. Basic economics tells us that the more abundant something is, the less value it holds. If everyone has easy access to it, like sand or shells commonly found on any beach, it cannot serve as an effective measure of value.

Around 770 BC, the first metal coins were created in China. As a nod to the past, the Chinese crafted miniature versions of tools once used as currency but gave them a practical update: the coins were made circular for easy handling, allowing people to reach into their pockets without injuring their fingers. They cast the coins in bronze, a material that couldn't simply be picked up on a beach—it was scarce and therefore valuable.

At this point, money wasn't yet an illusion. The value of a coin was directly tied to the value of the metal it was made from. A coin containing 1 gram of gold was worth exactly 1 gram of gold, a value you could measure and verify. However, kings and rulers soon recognized the power of money. They realized that amassing more of these tiny pieces of precious metal meant wielding greater control and influence.

In 600 BC, King Alyattes of Lydia established the first official money mint. He created coins from a mix of silver and gold, stamping each with an image to signify its denomination. This made it easier for people to identify the value of a coin at a glance. But the demand for more money quickly outpaced the supply of precious metals, which were costly to produce. To solve this, rulers began thinning the coins and diluting the expensive metals with cheaper ones.

Before long, the coins in circulation were worth less than the value stamped on their surface. This marked the beginning of the illusion of money—a system where the perceived value of currency no longer matched its material worth.

The value of a coin was no longer tied to the worth of the metal it contained. Instead, its value became whatever rulers and banks declared it to be. For example, one British pound sterling initially represented one pound of sterling silver. However, as international trade expanded, people realized that metal coins were too heavy and cumbersome for long-distance transactions.

In response, kings began issuing IOU certificates for trade. These pieces of paper, stamped with the royal seal, were trusted because people believed they could be redeemed for their equivalent value in coins. And for a while, that trust held true. But as these IOU certificates became more widespread, coins were needed less and less. Eventually, the paper itself held value, not because it could be exchanged for gold or silver, but because people believed in its worth.

From ancient monarchs to modern governments and central banks, money has always been an illusion—a symbol whose value depends entirely on the trust and importance people assign to it. Today, the most valuable banknote in circulation is the 10,000 Singapore dollar note. Although no longer produced, this single piece of paper—currently valued at 7,345 US dollars—remains legal tender. It can still be used to purchase valuable items like houses, cars, and even gold and silver.

The production cost of a banknote is less than 20 cents, yet under the fiat currency system, it is imbued with a value equivalent to 120 grams of gold. The term "fiat" refers to the modern monetary system, deriving from the Latin word meaning "let it be done." In essence, it signifies a government decree that establishes the value of money and enforces it as legal tender.

The concept of fiat money is a pervasive illusion, rarely questioned in daily life. However, just as ancient kings understood the power of currency, modern governments recognize its significance and continually seek more of it. Their solution? They can simply create more money out of thin air. For instance, if the United States government needed $340 million to purchase an F-22 jet, it could print the required amount.

The problem with this approach is inflation. For money to retain its value, it must function as a reliable medium of exchange. This requires the money supply to align with the value of goods and services in the economy. When too much money is created without a corresponding increase in goods and services, prices rise, and the currency's value diminishes.

This concern about inflation and monetary stability is why many economists—and everyday individuals—are worried about the state of the global reserve currency, the U.S. dollar. The years 2020 to 2023 were especially challenging globally, as the COVID-19 pandemic forced economies to shut down, exacerbating these financial pressures.

The availability of goods and services and the overall output of the economy were significantly reduced, slowing to a mere trickle, and the world seemed to come to a standstill for a while. With less money circulating to sustain the economy and prevent a complete collapse, the U.S. government began printing money at an unprecedented rate. In fact, 45% of all U.S. dollars in existence today were printed in 2020 alone. This is staggering, especially since the country's economic output hasn't increased significantly during this time. As a result, the prices of goods and services are likely to rise sharply.

This trend is already evident in the prices of commodities like lumber, which has tripled in cost compared to just a year ago. You might have also noticed subtle price increases at your favourite restaurants—perhaps the dosa at the street shop costs 5 to 10 rupees more than it did last year. These changes are happening quietly, right under our noses.

On the surface, government stimulus and unemployment checks may seem like a positive response. They provide much-needed relief to those struggling the most, which is undoubtedly beneficial. However, this approach is a double-edged sword. While it offers short-term assistance, the long-term implications could include rising inflation and other economic challenges.

We have reached a point where, due to inflation and a slowing economy, people struggle to find the right jobs at the right time. Often, it's not because they don't want to work, but because the available jobs are simply less favourable than the alternatives.

Take India as an example: daily wage workers aren't legally entitled to a guaranteed minimum wage. For waitstaff, most of their income comes from tips rather than wages. If businesses can't hire the staff they need to operate, they risk shutting down—it's a domino effect. But what can be done? When unemployment benefits and stimulus checks pay more than some jobs, there's little incentive for people to seek employment in the first place.

The Federal Reserve in the United States plays a subtle yet powerful role in this situation. It essentially allows the government to create money out of thin air and inject it into the economy without drawing too much public attention. This approach, while providing temporary relief, raises concerns about long-term sustainability.

Before 2020, the United States had accumulated a staggering $29 trillion in debt—an almost unimaginable sum. This debt is issued through bonds and treasury notes, which are essentially promises from the government to pay a specified amount, along with interest.

Right now, 10 years U.S. treasury bond will return you 1.23 percent on your investment at expiry. So if you put it 1000 dollar today, you will have made 12.30 percent by 2031. That sounds terrible already, but to add the icing on the cake, it doesn't even keep up with inflation, which is targeted to stay at around 2% of a year. It is a lot higher than that, but that's for another time. By investing in government notes of your own country, which issues the currency you use everyday, you actually lose buying power over a decade. It is weakened by the day.

But regardless, banks, business, and individuals around the world buy these bonds and treasury notes and the government uses all that money it gets back how it sees fit. However, when it's time for the government to pay its debt, all the money they made has been spent. So they buy back all the treasuries and bonds, but only from the big financial institutions, and the pay them back with new money created out of thin air. Since march 2020, the federal reserve has bought back over 1 trillion dollar in bonds, and is planning to continue to do so far the foreseeable future.

While this process injects liquidity into the economy and generates more interest income, it also increases the money supply, which diminishes the value of each dollar. Multi-trillion-dollar stimulus payments and infrastructure packages only exacerbate this trend, raising questions about how long such practices can continue.

Every time new money is created, it erodes the value of existing money. The balance in your bank account may not change, but its purchasing power steadily declines. In essence, holding wealth in fiat currencies like the U.S. dollar means that your money is constantly being devalued. Over time, you will find that your savings buy less and less, making it increasingly challenging to preserve your wealth.

The reality that money is nothing, but an illusion is one that we must all embrace. Because only then will the path to financial freedom become clearer. It is all a game, a game that never truly ends. Understanding that money does not have any intrinsic value in itself, but instead only inherits the value we give to it, will prevent you from trying to store up your wealth in currency.

Instead, using that money to acquire assets that appreciate faster than inflation is the only way to win the game. And it is not really winning, it is avoiding total loss. As more money is printed each and every day, the value of each dollar in your pocket will continue to decrease, but the dollar value of assets around the globe will continue to appreciate in value. But it is all a mirage, it is some and mirrors.

The stock market, which seems to be in perpetual "up only" mode, might give the illusion that everything is fine—but it's not. It's all measured in a currency that is slowly losing value every single day. What is the ultimate endgame here? With fiat currencies and an unlimited supply of money, will their value simply keep declining indefinitely? Will the gap between the rich and poor continue to widen? Or will we finally address a problem as old as humanity itself and take control of our financial future instead of leaving it in the hands of those who erode it daily? Only time will tell—but remember, there is a way out.

ÞÞÞ

TEN

THE PERCEPTION OF MONEY

Those who understand the importance of saving recognize the beauty of money, but those who grasp its true value unlock the path to wealth. How is that possible when everyone is earning the same currency? We've often heard friends and parents advise us to save money so we can afford whatever we desire—but is that really true? For many entrepreneurs, this mindset becomes the foundation of their unwavering belief and vision for success. The answers are right before our eyes; we just need to see them clearly. Do you see it now?

A boy born in Gujarat found himself working at a Shell petrol station in Yemen due to his family's circumstances. There, he noticed something unusual: the country's coins were rich in silver. He began melting these coins and selling the silver to merchants in London for a profit. With the money he earned, he returned to India and started a spice and textile business. That boy was none other than Dhirubhai Ambani. Through his strategies and skills, he became the richest person in India. Ambani meticulously studied Indian laws and exploited legal loopholes to propel his company to extraordinary heights. He deeply understood that the true value of money lies not in the currency itself but in the assets and opportunities it can create.

The game of money in this world is indeed peculiar. It doesn't always favor those with the best training, connections, or education—sometimes, it's the one who starts with nothing who overcomes the odds. While luck plays a role, understanding finance is even more crucial. Financial literacy is a powerful skill, yet many of us remain unaware of how money operates in our daily lives.

We often treat money like a rigid science—bound by rules, regulations, and fixed principles. However, money is more like a psychological subject, deeply influenced by our emotions and decisions. Science deals with absolutes and predictable outcomes, but money behaves differently; it fluctuates based on individual habits and choices. It's a dynamic force shaped by how we think, feel, and act.

The worlds expensive thing is trust, because it is very in demand and sell supply.

In Rich Dad Poor Dad, Robert Kiyosaki explains that while the poor and middle class work for money, the rich make money work for them—a statement that holds undeniable truth. Interestingly, the more we earn, the more we tend to spend. But why is that?

In 1982, there was a man who had no money in hand and no idea about his next job. Yet, within just a decade, he became someone who paid more income tax than even Ambani. However, by 2002, the same man tragically passed away as a prisoner, sitting alone in a government hospital chair, with no one by his side.

His life took a remarkable turn while working as a humble cashier at New India Assurance Company. Starting out as an ordinary employee under a boss, he began learning how the stock market operated. In time, he climbed to a position where he could establish his own business. He closely studied the stock market and observed how certain individuals seemed to influence when a stock would rise or fall.

He noticed a pattern: when a company raised the prices of its products, sales would naturally decline. This, in turn, often caused the company's stock value to drop in the market. He realized that holding a significant number of shares in such a company during a price hike could lead to losses. However, by predicting when a company was likely to increase its prices, one could sell their shares at a high price before the decline, securing a profit.

Though this strategy might lead to losses for buyers, it ensured profits for sellers—an unwritten but undeniable truth of the stock market.

Harshad Mehta, known as the "Big Bull" of the stock market, had an intricate web of connections. He had key executives from various companies in his pocket, ensuring he received insider information about their decisions before they became public. Using this privileged knowledge, he strategically bought and sold stocks. Not only that, but he also sought to learn about events like impending strikes in these companies. Mehta realized that if a company halted production, its sales would inevitably drop. Anticipating such scenarios, he would sell related stocks in advance to secure profits.

But his tactics didn't stop there. Imagine someone rents a small room, registers it as a company, and lists a few hundred shares under its name. Over the next ten days, the value of these shares starts to climb steadily. As the shares continue to trade, their prices rise gradually. Curious investors, mistaking it for a legitimate new company, begin purchasing these stocks. Suddenly, the prices skyrocket, and the company becomes the talk of the market. When the stock value reaches its peak, Mehta would sell off all his holdings, leaving others wondering what happened. The truth would only emerge later—that the company never existed.

In February 1991, the Bombay Stock Exchange (BSE) index was at 1,000 points. Within a year, it soared to 4,500 points—a staggering growth in such a short period. Despite his manipulative schemes, the public perceived Harshad Mehta as a visionary who had accurately predicted and capitalized on the market's growth. However, his greed for even greater profits soon attracted the attention of journalists and investigators.

It eventually came to light that Mehta had paid bribes, including a ₹1 crore bribe to then Prime Minister P.V. Narasimha Rao, to further his schemes. His unchecked ambition and unethical practices ultimately exposed the dark side of his success and shook the financial world.

We often earn money without truly needing it, yet once we have it, we find ourselves wanting more. In the game of making money, it's not about how well you play—it's about when you decide to stop. If you win and then lose, the loss becomes your legacy. But if you start and succeed, that victory will be remembered in history.

Because "History only remember how you finished"

Vijay Mallya, Mehul Choksi, Nirav Modi—have you ever wondered why the Indian government has been unable to bring these individuals to justice, despite strong diplomatic ties with other nations? When the wealthy commit even the most unforgivable offenses, they often use their money to cover up their mistakes. But what about the common people?

Take the example of Shah Rukh Khan's son, who was arrested for drug use. If he were still in jail, we would still be talking about it today. However, Shah Rukh Khan bailed him out, and as a result, the incident has faded from public memory. This is the difference money makes—it has the power to rewrite narratives and erase consequences.

"History never repeat twice, but man always does"

Seventy percent of people in the world share similar thoughts about money. However, the percentage of those who not only think but take action is remarkably small. These individuals base their decisions on events and experiences accumulated between their twenties and fifties. This highlights that no one is inherently foolish or exceptionally intelligent—it's all about perspective and action.

Bill Gates once said: Success is a lousy teacher, it seduces smart people into thinking they can't lose. But how about failure, it is also a lousy teacher, to seduce failures into thinking they will lose.

We can't dismiss the value of wrong decisions, as sometimes, ten wrong choices can lead us to one right decision in life. A beggar seeks food, while a middle-class person with enough to eat aspires to buy a bike. The bike owner dreams of owning a car, the car owner wishes for higher social status, those with status aim to become millionaires, and millionaires aspire to be billionaires. Desire keeps pushing us forward—just think about how far it can take us.

We all have a desire to earn money, but many of us lack an understanding of how money truly works. A common misconception is that success in business comes easily, but without a solid grasp of its fundamentals, it's impossible to succeed.

For example, many people regularly invest in the stock market without fully understanding it. We buy shares and assume that's the end of it, without considering what happens behind the scenes—how profits are generated, where our investment goes, and how the financial cycle operates.

By understanding these mechanisms, we gain clarity on how to make informed decisions—knowing when to invest, which shares to buy, and when to sell. With this knowledge, achieving consistent profits becomes much easier.

How can we avoid wasting money? If you believe that simply working hard to earn money, building a house, or buying property to save money is the wisest approach, you might be mistaken.

The wealthy typically don't buy a house, especially at the start of their journey to success. Instead, they rent a home while focusing on building assets that can eventually afford them that same house.

One of the biggest mistakes many people make is taking on significant debt to buy a house. This can be financially destructive, as it often involves tying up all your assets, savings, and additional borrowed money into one investment. This approach is risky, as owning a house doesn't generate income—on the contrary, it incurs ongoing expenses unless you rent it out.

That's not to say owning a home to share with your family is wrong. The real problem lies in purchasing a house with excessive debt, which can gradually lead to financial ruin.

Don't pay for a gym membership unless you're truly committed. Statistics show that in 2017, about 61 million people were gym members, but nearly 70% of students with memberships stopped using them after the first few months. Many gyms count on people paying their fees without actually showing up.

People often join gyms to improve their health and fitness, as gyms provide a variety of equipment and classes. However, joining a gym without a strong commitment to regular exercise is ineffective. A gym membership is pointless if it's not used consistently.

Instead, consider smarter, low-cost or free fitness options. Outdoor activities like walking, playing sports, running, or hiking are great alternatives. Train your mind to stay persistent and develop discipline before committing to a formal exercise routine.

Don't buy luxury items if you won't use them. Many people make the mistake of purchasing things they don't need, regardless of the price. While millionaires can afford mansions, luxury cars, designer clothes, and other expensive items, it doesn't mean they spend their hard-earned money recklessly on material possessions. They can acquire such things in abundance, yet you'll often see them wearing simple watches worth ₹2000 or using the same phone for years.

It's important to evaluate whether such purchases are truly the best choice. For instance, consider whether it's better to spend ₹1000 to ₹1500 on a simple luxury brand T-shirt or opt for a T-shirt of similar quality for ₹350 to ₹500, minus the brand logo. Often, the only difference is the label, not the quality.

Avoid buying a new car unless it's absolutely necessary. Purchasing a brand-new car is one of the worst financial decisions many people make, especially younger generations. The reason? As soon as you drive the car off the dealership lot, it begins to depreciate. By the end of the first year, the car's value typically drops by 20% to 30%, and after five years, it will have lost at least 60% of its original value.

Many people take out loans to buy new cars, essentially borrowing money to purchase an asset that loses value rapidly. However, it's not all bad news. If you want the experience of driving a shiny, nearly-new car without taking on debt, consider buying a used car that's two or three years old. These vehicles are often in excellent condition, and you can purchase them at a significant discount—typically around 30% less than their original price—thanks to their initial depreciation.

Avoid spending money on luxury TVs or video games. Middle-class and lower-income households often waste time and money on these activities, far more than wealthier households. First, there's the cost of acquiring the latest TV packages or gaming systems. Then, there's the lost time spent on activities like gaming or binge-watching, which could instead be used for more productive pursuits, such as learning new skills or exploring ways to generate additional income.

For instance, individuals from higher-income households are more likely to spend their free time reading books, which contributes to their personal growth and financial knowledge. In contrast, many people from lower-income groups tend to use their leisure time watching Netflix or other streaming services, missing opportunities for self-improvement and wealth creation.

Isn't it hard for us when a book advises us not to waste time and to focus on what comes next? Don't worry, this advice is all about earning money and achieving success in life, and for many, it brings happiness. But it's not meant for those who feel like they're falling behind in life. One concerning thing is that many people don't realize that the money we have now is not something permanent.

Pay close attention to what I'm about to explain.

Don't spend your money on single utility device!

Many of us enjoy collecting watches, but when you think about it, whether it's a 500-rupee watch or a 5000-rupee watch, both serve the same purpose of telling the time. Also like watches, like shoes, these are the single utility product. There is no necessary to spend more money on it.

Always invest your money in assets, like land, like gold, stocks, bonds.

Don't invest your money in liabilities, like buildings, car, bike.

Remember, they way to build wealth is not only saving your money.

ନ୍ଦନ୍ଦନ୍ଦ

ELEVEN

The Perception of Corporate World

The corporate world operates on a set of unwritten rules and dynamics that often resemble the unpredictable nature of a dream. Much like how events in dreams unfold without our control, the workplace can feel like a space where things happen beyond our expectations, and at times, beyond our influence. While we may not be able to control every element of this environment, we can certainly navigate it with intention and strategic foresight, making sure we master the visible world—the workplace dynamics and relationships—around us.

Entering the corporate world can feel like stepping into a new dimension, where power structures, expectations, and competition all intertwine. One of the key elements in thriving within this space is understanding that it's not always about being the most knowledgeable or the hardest worker. In fact, presenting yourself as someone who doesn't have all the answers can sometimes be the most strategic move.

In a workplace, especially early on, it's wise to avoid appearing overly confident in your knowledge or abilities. If a question arises and you genuinely don't know the answer, it's okay to say "I don't know"—but only when necessary. This approach prevents you from overcommitting to tasks or responsibilities that you might not be able to deliver on. By acknowledging your limits, you avoid the risk of burning out or overloading yourself. It also creates an opportunity to learn from others, allowing you to build relationships and leverage the expertise of your colleagues, which can ultimately lead to more success in the long run.

Delegation is a critical aspect of navigating the corporate environment. Many employees, especially those early in their careers, feel the need to prove themselves by taking on every task thrown their way. While enthusiasm and a strong work ethic are valuable, trying to do everything yourself can lead to inefficiency. The workplace is not about doing everything alone; it's about knowing who can help and when to ask for support. Effective delegation allows you to focus on high-priority tasks, manage your workload efficiently, and build teamwork. The more you rely on others for support, the better you can focus on your core strengths and contribute more meaningfully to the organization.

Moreover, the corporate world can be a highly competitive space. It's not always enough to simply do the work—you must also manage how the work is perceived. This often includes ensuring that credit is given where it's due, but also protecting your own contributions. In competitive environments, there's always the risk that someone else might claim credit for your ideas or efforts. While it might seem underhanded, taking credit for others' work can be a strategic move in certain contexts. This doesn't necessarily mean stealing someone else's idea outright, but it could involve subtly influencing how credit is allocated or positioning yourself as the face of a project.

A classic example of this phenomenon can be seen in the story of Nikola Tesla, whose groundbreaking work on the dynamo is often overshadowed by the legacy of Thomas Edison. While Tesla spent long hours—sometimes 17 to 18 hours a day—working on revolutionary ideas, Edison capitalized on those innovations, earning much of the credit for them. Tesla's story illustrates how contributions can be overlooked, while those who manage to claim ownership of the work—fairly or unfairly—reap the rewards. In this competitive landscape, it's not only the quality of your work that counts but also how you position that work in the eyes of others.

Similarly, many politicians, speakers, and leaders borrow ideas or words from historical figures, reworking them into their own speeches or platforms. It's an open secret in the world of public speaking and politics: leveraging the wisdom of others and reframing it in your own way can often create a powerful, compelling message, even though the original idea may not have been yours. This doesn't necessarily devalue the speaker's efforts; it's a strategy used to build credibility, connect with audiences, and position oneself as knowledgeable or visionary.

In many industries, simply completing the tasks assigned to you is not enough. You must be adept at ensuring that your contributions are recognized and credited. In fact, it's not just about completing the work—it's about claiming your due recognition for that work. If you don't actively protect your contributions, there's a real risk that someone else will benefit from your labor—whether it's a colleague who takes credit for your ideas, a manager who overlooks your accomplishments, or a competitor who positions themselves as the sole driving force behind a successful project.

The corporate world often rewards those who can master both the technical aspects of their job and the politics of recognition. It's about understanding that the game is not always fair, and those who succeed are often those who know how to play the game strategically, balancing effort with visibility.

In essence, the workplace is not just about working hard—it's about navigating the social and professional dynamics to ensure your hard work doesn't go unnoticed. Whether it's delegating tasks, claiming credit, or leveraging the work of others, the ability to position yourself strategically can make all the difference in climbing the corporate ladder and achieving long-term success.

In the corporate world, you are replaceable!

A close acquaintance of mine had dedicated 17 years of his life to a multinational company, putting in countless hours and giving his best effort each day. After all those years, when he finally received an offer from another prestigious company with a significantly higher salary, he decided to take the plunge and submit his resignation. To his surprise, there was no counteroffer, no plea for him to stay, and within days, someone else was brought in to fill his position.

This scenario is a stark reminder of the harsh reality of the corporate world: work never stops, and the organization doesn't stop because of any individual. No matter how long you've been with a company or how much you've contributed, in the end, you are replaceable. If you're gone, the company will continue on without you. While some colleagues or superiors may check in on you during personal struggles or sickness as a polite gesture, few will go beyond that. The truth is, your recovery time doesn't affect the company's operations, and kindness often takes a back seat to efficiency and productivity.

This is not to say that people aren't valuable, but rather, the organization's needs and bottom line take precedence over individual circumstances. In a corporate environment, it's important to understand that loyalty is a one-sided relationship; the company's resources and infrastructure are designed to continue operating smoothly with or without your presence. This understanding is key to navigating your career—because while you may be irreplaceable in your own eyes, the company can easily find someone else to fill your shoes.

Another insight from the corporate world is that sometimes, it's best not to act too hastily when facing a situation. For example, when you approach a manager about an issue, they might dismiss your concern—not because they don't understand or care about it, but because they believe addressing it immediately might make the situation worse. Sometimes, waiting for the right moment is part of a broader strategy.

At first glance, this approach may seem frustrating. You might feel that had the manager acted sooner, the problem could have been resolved more smoothly, without the confusion or escalation that followed. However, from the manager's perspective, there is often a deeper reasoning. By waiting, they can ensure that their involvement is more visible, demonstrating their leadership and problem-solving capabilities when it becomes more evident that their intervention is necessary. The delayed resolution allows them to step in as the "savior," highlighting their value to the organization. In this way, timing can be used as a tool to ensure that their contributions are recognized when it truly counts.

This example also ties into another important lesson: doing good work is not always enough. While your job may require you to complete tasks to the best of your ability, the key to career advancement often lies in visibility. Many colleagues in any workplace may perform exceptionally well but still find themselves underappreciated during appraisals. Why? Because it's not just about doing the work—it's about making sure the work you do is recognized and acknowledged.

In an ideal world, merit would be the sole factor determining your compensation and career progression. But in reality, how well you promote your contributions is just as crucial. It's not enough to simply complete your responsibilities behind the scenes; you need to make your impact known to those who matter. The work itself is only part of the equation; the other part is ensuring that the people who are in a position to reward you can clearly see the value you bring to the table.

In the corporate world, success often depends not just on your ability to do the job but on how effectively you position yourself, your achievements, and your contributions. It's about playing the game strategically finding the right balance between being indispensable and remaining visible.

Learn how to showcase your work!

Never assume you can outshine your manager, no matter how competent or talented you are. It may sound counterintuitive, especially in a competitive environment where individual performance often gets the spotlight, but attempts to impress your manager can backfire. While it's natural to want recognition for your contributions, it's important to recognize that your manager or those in higher authority are often the ones who need to be seen as the focal point. In a corporate environment, respect for authority and hierarchy is paramount, and it's essential to navigate the power dynamics with care.

High-ranking individuals typically expect to be at the center of attention, and by drawing excessive focus to yourself, you might unintentionally create friction. If your actions shift the spotlight away from them, they could feel sidelined, overlooked, or even threatened. This could be perceived as an attempt to undermine their position, which can lead to tensions. Your manager may see your behavior as a challenge to their authority, and if these feelings escalate, it could jeopardize your standing in the organization. The corporate world thrives on hierarchy, and while it's important to showcase your skills and accomplishments, it's crucial to do so without overshadowing the people who hold power over your career.

The key is finding balance: demonstrate your value, but never at the expense of others. It's perfectly acceptable to highlight your work, but be mindful of the context and how your actions might affect the dynamics of the workplace. Ensure your efforts to shine don't inadvertently diminish the influence of your manager or make them feel threatened.

In the corporate world, never openly oppose your manager. Your manager holds the ultimate authority in your work environment, and challenging them can lead to serious consequences. Even if you strongly disagree with a decision or strategy, outright opposition can be seen as disrespectful and insubordinate. In extreme cases, it may even put your job in jeopardy. Managers are typically responsible for the team's performance, and when you challenge their decisions publicly or in front of others, it can undermine their position and cause rifts.

It's important to understand that there may be times when your manager is not fully aware of the intricacies of your work. They might be unfamiliar with specific details or processes, and while your intention may be to help them by offering clarification, this can be perceived as undermining their authority. Even if you're genuinely trying to offer advice or guidance, it's essential to approach these situations tactfully. Any attempt to "teach" your manager in front of others can create resentment, so it's always wiser to communicate in a private setting where your intention can be more clearly understood.

If you find yourself in a situation where your manager has made a mistake, resist the urge to point it out immediately in a public setting. Publicly embarrassing a superior can have serious repercussions. Instead, wait for a more appropriate moment—perhaps a private discussion where you can address the issue respectfully. Pointing out a mistake in a one-on-one, calm conversation not only shows professionalism but also helps maintain the respect and trust between you and your manager. It's a way of maintaining a constructive approach to resolving issues without inflaming any negative emotions.

In any professional setting, it's also essential to avoid becoming too personally attached to your manager. While developing a rapport or friendly relationship with your boss may seem like a good idea at first, it can quickly become a double-edged sword. Personal attachment to your manager may blur the lines between professional and personal boundaries, leading to complex dynamics that could negatively impact your career.

For instance, if a personal relationship forms and you make a mistake at work, your manager's reaction may be more severe than expected. The emotional complexity of the relationship might influence their judgment, and they may react with frustration or disappointment that wouldn't occur if you had maintained a strictly professional relationship. This could lead to awkwardness and tension, both in the workplace and within the manager-employee relationship.

Having a personal attachment with your manager might feel rewarding in the moment, but it can also create unforeseen complications. If you make an error or face challenges at work, it can be much more difficult to maintain the same level of professionalism in your interactions. The emotional dynamics at play might cloud your judgment or your manager's response, and what might have been a minor issue could escalate unnecessarily.

Ultimately, having a healthy boundary between personal and professional relationships is key. While building a strong, respectful relationship with your manager is important, it's equally essential to keep your professional identity intact. By avoiding excessive attachment, you protect yourself from potential pitfalls and ensure that you maintain the necessary professionalism to succeed in the workplace.

Personal attachment sometimes will go against the situation! Having a personal relationship with your manager creates a bond that can, at times, become potentially harmful to you.

The truth is: "People join the company but leave their manager."

Avoid gossiping with anyone in your office—it's a common mistake that can have far-reaching consequences. In the workplace, gossip often feels like a harmless way to bond with colleagues or share opinions, but it can quickly spiral into something more damaging. When we gossip, we often lose sight of the bigger picture and fail to consider the potential fallout. Sharing personal opinions about others or engaging in negative talk can backfire, leaving you vulnerable to reputational damage.

One of the key risks of office gossip is the chance that someone you confide in may hold a different agenda. If a colleague perceives you as an obstacle to their growth or sees an opportunity to undermine you, they might use what you've said as leverage. It's easy for them to twist your words or expose your gossip to others, potentially making your name the focal point of office discussions. Suddenly, you're no longer seen as a neutral or trustworthy colleague, but someone who engages in behind-the-scenes talk. This could create unnecessary tension, mistrust, and gossip about your actions, which could ultimately impact your work and relationships at the company.

Another potential issue arises when you speak negatively about yourself, even if it's meant in jest. Self-deprecating humor may seem harmless, but it can be easily misinterpreted. Colleagues might not realize you're joking or might take your negative statements seriously. If you regularly downplay your strengths or abilities, others might start to view you as insecure, which could affect how they perceive your professional competence. Instead of boosting your likability, self-deprecating comments can diminish your perceived value in the workplace, even if that's not your intention.

Moreover, remember that if you talk about others in the office, the person you're confiding in is likely to gossip about you when you're not around. Even if you trust a colleague, they may feel compelled to share what you've said, either to seek validation or simply out of habit. It's important to remember that office conversations can be easily twisted, and once something is said, it can be challenging to take it back. What you share today might come back to haunt you tomorrow.

To avoid the pitfalls of gossip, it's crucial to maintain a level of professionalism and discretion at all times. Stay focused on your work and the tasks at hand, and engage with colleagues in a way that fosters collaboration, not division. If you feel the urge to discuss something personal or share your thoughts, consider doing so outside the workplace or in a setting where the stakes are lower. By avoiding gossip, you protect both your reputation and the integrity of your relationships within the office.

Always remember: "The people who gossip with you, gossip about you."

ᑭᑭᑭ

TWELVE

THE PERCEPTION OF PERCEPTION

What happens when we view a perspective from another angle? How many different perspectives can the human mind generate?

Some argue that accepting criticism helps us recognize and correct our mistakes, while others believe that doing so may hinder our progress.

In this world, we often deem taking a life to be wrong, yet it is the same individuals who take life to sustain their own.

We often say that God created life in this world, but now humans can create life artificially. Does that mean we should start calling humans God?

Our parents often tell us not to talk to strangers, yet we end up marrying one.

When we need medical treatment, we are told to see a doctor, but if that doctor needs treatment, will they treat themselves or seek help from another doctor? If they can't save themselves, how can they save others?

In this world, it is just as difficult to be weak as it is to be strong.

Life is always a new beginning, which is why we are encouraged to forget old memories. Yet, at the same time, we move forward in life shaped by those very memories and past experiences.

Many people claim they should always be alone in life, yet at the same time, they also say that friends, love, and relationships are essential.

We often say that lending money to others can ruin a relationship, yet when we're in need, we ask our close ones for a loan. Are we implying that asking for help can end the relationship?

We are often told not to dwell on our emotions, yet we believe that true strength in life comes only when we face pain.

We often say that if you encounter someone smarter than you, it's better to collaborate with them rather than compete, as competition is a sign of weakness. Yet, at the same time, we believe that we can improve and grow by competing with others.

We are told to remain silent in every situation, yet we also believe that speaking up is the only way to resolve an issue.

While the law deems it a crime to harm animals or humans, at the same time, we justify killing animals or humans for our own protection.

We're advised never to change ourselves for anyone or anything, but at the same time, we're told that growth comes only when we adapt ourselves to the circumstances and the times.

We are told not to share our personal matters with others, yet we also say that sharing them brings peace of mind.

We believe that progress comes from facing the obstacles ahead, but we also say that ignoring the signs is the key to advancement.

Both men and women experience failure in love, so why do singers often portray men as the only ones vulnerable?

We're advised not to get too close to our manager at work, yet we also hear that being close to your manager can lead to a promotion.

We often say that happiness in life comes from earning more money, yet at the same time, we claim that more money won't bring happiness or peace.

What seems right today may be wrong tomorrow, as the world around us is constantly evolving. This dynamic nature of life ensures that nothing is truly permanent; everything—whether it's our surroundings, relationships, or even our own thoughts—changes with time and shifting circumstances. What we believe to be true or just in one moment might be contradicted by new experiences, new information, or altered perspectives in the future. As humans, we often find ourselves navigating through life without clear answers to what is permanent and what is fleeting, because our understanding is fluid, influenced by our evolving views and the unpredictable nature of the world.

In relationships and social interactions, we may experience moments where we feel misunderstood or mocked by others, believing it to be an unfair judgment of our character. However, it's interesting how we sometimes justify similar actions when we are the ones making fun of others. In those instances, we may convince ourselves that mocking others brings us happiness or a sense of superiority, not realizing that this behavior may be rooted in insecurity or the need to elevate ourselves at someone else's expense.

Our perspectives shift in response to our circumstances, meaning that our views are not fixed but are adaptable depending on the situation at hand. We often do not pause to evaluate whether our perspective is right or wrong, instead simply allowing it to be shaped by our immediate context, emotions, and the experiences we are facing. This malleability in thought can be both a strength and a weakness, as it allows us to adapt to change but can also lead us to act impulsively without fully considering the consequences. In the end, it highlights the impermanence and subjectivity of our beliefs, urging us to recognize that the world is fluid, and our views may not always be as absolute as we think.

We admire it when we hear that someone has lived for over 100 years. But in reality, do we truly think that they've lived all those years, or are we simply acknowledging that they haven't passed away yet?

ppp

THIRTEEN

THE PERCEPTION OF WHY?

Often, we fail to understand the perspective in front of us. These are things that happen in our everyday lives. What kind of thoughts or questions do we have that everyone else also shares?

We wake up in the morning, take a clean bath, and tidy up our space. But why does the towel get dirty?

In school, we refer to someone as a teacher if they specialize in one subject. But why do we call someone a student if they are expected to know every subject?

If our dreams reflect what we do and experience in real life, then why don't we dream about using our mobile phones?

We often advise against drinking and driving, so why is there bike parking in front of the bar?

When we yell at the deaf, do they think we are yelling?

Why do we commonly write with a blue pen?

A, B, C, D are different letters, so why do we say they should be in alphabetical order?

We are eligible to vote in elections at the age of 18 and to get married at 23. So, does marriage require more responsibility than electing a country's prime minister?

If the soap slips down, will the place it falls on get clean, or will the soap get dirty?

If there is no charge in the battery, why do we hit the remote?

In the process of cleaning one thing, we end up dirtying another.

In a numerical sequence, 12 follows 11, so why does 11 AM come after 12 AM?

If we want to sleep, we have to pretend to sleep first.

If a building catches fire and everyone flees, if I were inside taking a shower at that moment, would the fire be on us?

We have air around us, and without air, we would die. Fish are surrounded by water; without water, the fish die. We can't see air, so fish can't see water?

A birthday means we are getting old, and we will die soon. So, if we are going to die soon, then we should say "birthday" sadly. Why do we say it happily?

We drink to forget everything, but why do we visit a doctor for amnesia if we are forgetting things automatically?

We feel sad when our faces darken, and we also feel sad when our hair turns white.

The miracle is that the brain is the only thing that names itself as the brain.

After we die, we are laid to rest in a graveyard. But is our stomach the graveyard for goats and chickens?

The brain commands the heart to beat, yet the heart pumps blood to help the brain function. So, does the brain depend on the heart, or does the heart depend on the brain?

Isn't it only when we bite our tongues that we truly realize how hard we bite the food?

When a YouTube video struggles to play due to a low-quality network, how do advertisements play in high quality without buffering?

In this world, why is it that we can't ignore words we see without reading them?

Why don't we adjust the clock when it shows the wrong time, yet we adjust ourselves according to the clock's time?

In my life, I haven't seen any Micro Owen advertisements on TV or social media. Why?

When we hear shocking news, we stand while sitting, and we sit while standing. Why?

Why aren't the alphabetical words in order on the keyboard?

Here, every store does not allow civilians to enter without wearing a mask. But we need to step into the store to buy a mask. How?

When we receive a call while riding, we say we're stuck in traffic. But we don't realize that we are the traffic.

Is the snake's head long, or is its body long?

The venom is in the snake's head. So, if the snake unknowingly bites itself, will the venom spread throughout its body and cause it to die?

The throat of the giraffe is very long, so does it take a long time for the vomit to reach it?

If you reach the age of 35, then all the dogs in the world may have been born after you, right?

After a doctor treats a patient, the patient says, "Doctor, you have saved my life." But did the doctor really save his life or just postpone his death?

Is our smile caused when we breathe fast?

When soft things spoil, they turn hard. But when hard things spoil, they turn soft and fluffy.

Your bike key has traveled more than your bike. Isn't it?

Do children born deaf perceive the world as being very quiet?

A vacuum cleaner at home is dirty. If we clean it, then we are vacuuming the cleaner ourselves, right?

Is the orange fruit called "orange" because of its color, or is the color orange named after the fruit?

If we lock two mind readers in a single room, one person will read the other's mind, and then the other will read the first person's mind. In the end, whose mind will be read by whom?

Before the discovery of the phone, no one might have asked, "Where are you?" right?

Do blind people turn off the lights at night?

All the animals outside the ear give birth. All the animals inside the ear lay eggs, don't they?

Are humans the only ones who pay money to live in this world?

You know the answers to all of these. If yes, I'm happy for you!

ᛒᛒᛒ

Summary

Everything we do, every thought we've had, is produced by the human brain. But exactly how it operates remains one of the biggest unsolved mysteries, and it seems the more we probe its secrets, the more surprises we find.

At times in life, we find ourselves questioning why certain events occur and what their purpose might be. Some people feel the need to understand these reasons, believing that someone—either directly or indirectly—must have guided them to that understanding. Just as we need light to see the world around us, many of us tend to believe only what we see, hear, and speak. It can be challenging to comprehend the deeper meanings of the ever-changing elements of this world. Some believe that the universe exists to satisfy their own desires, while others think that we were created to serve a greater purpose in helping the universe fulfill its mission.

The Perception: Bring it to Light is a thought-provoking exploration of how perception shapes our understanding of the world, ourselves, and the relationships we build. This book delves into the intricate processes of how we interpret reality, exposing the unseen filters—emotions, beliefs, experiences, and societal norms—that influence our thoughts, actions, and decisions.

Far from being just an intellectual study, the book challenges readers to question the norms they've accepted, uncover hidden perspectives, and reflect on how their views are formed and transformed. It encourages self-awareness, inviting readers to bring clarity to the overlooked corners of their minds and redefine their realities.

Through this journey, The Perception: Bring it to Light empowers readers to see beyond surface appearances, embrace a deeper understanding of themselves and the world, and live authentically. It's not just a book; it's a guide to unlocking the power of perception and creating a life aligned with clarity, purpose, and truth.

"All the best for your Perception"

ᗐᗐᗐ

9 7 9 8 8 9 6 7 3 0 0 5 7